CHRIS PACKHAM

AMAZING ANIMAL
HOMES

ILLUSTRATED BY JASON COCKCROFT

First published in Great Britain 2018 by Red Shed,
an imprint of Egmont UK Limited
The Yellow Building, 1 Nicholas Road
London W11 4AN

www.egmont.co.uk

Text copyright © Chris Packham 2018
Illustrations copyright © Jason Cockcroft 2018

The author and illustrator hereby assert their moral rights.

ISBN 978 1 4052 8489 9

A CIP catalogue record for this book is available from the British Library.

Stay safe online. Any website addresses listed in this book are correct at the time of going
to print. However, Egmont is not responsible for content hosted by third parties. Please be
aware that online content can be subject to change and websites can contain content that
is unsuitable for children. We advise that all children are supervised when using the internet.

CHRIS PACKHAM

AMAZING ANIMAL
HOMES

ILLUSTRATED BY JASON COCKCROFT

RED
SHED

Like you, animals need a place to call home
where they can be safe and be a family.

barn owl

Some animals even move into our buildings.
These shelter them from the weather
and help them find food such as mice.

Others are born with ready-made homes,
or they find shells that they carry around
with them and can retreat into.

hermit crab

Some animals get together to form
an underwater colony, such as coral,
that grows and becomes their home.

coral

On land, trees offer an ideal place to rest in at night. And it's not just birds that make nests up high to keep out of the way of danger!

black-and-white ruffed lemur

Rocky caves are perfect hideaways for many different animals, both predator and prey. Did you know that our ancestors once lived in caves?

snow leopard

porcupine

Living underground is better for other animals.
They dig burrows and tunnels to keep warm or cool.
Would you like to see some other animal homes?

DARWIN'S BARK SPIDERS live by themselves and are very small, but they make the world's largest webs. They stretch their webs across wide rivers and lakes.

A spider spins silk into the air and this is carried
by the wind from one side of a river to the other.
Halfway along, it spins a different, sticky type of
silk into a huge wheel-shaped web to trap flies and
other insects that are flying above the water.

Thousands of **HONEY BEES** swarm together in hives, which they make inside tree hollows or caves. They produce wax that is used to make the cells of the honeycomb.

The honeycomb acts like a larder to store honey
that the bees make from nectar collected from flowers.
It also provides a safe nursery for the queen bee's eggs.

queen bee

AFRICAN TERMITES also live together in colonies. They build chimney-like mounds on top of their underground nests, which can be taller than a giraffe! The hard-working insects mix soil and their saliva together to make the mounds, which have lots of holes in them to let hot air escape from the nest below.

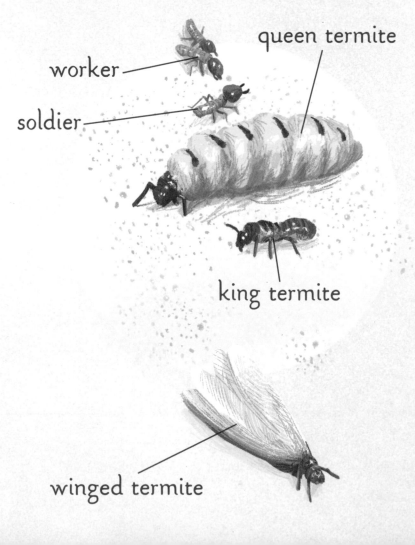

worker

soldier

queen termite

king termite

winged termite

Some of these termite homes, or 'termitariums',
are used for over a hundred years. They become
hard like cement, as car drivers find out when
they occasionally crash into them!

While some animals must work hard to make places to live, others have a 'mobile home' as part of their bodies. In North America, **GOPHER TORTOISES** are born with protective shells. When the temperature soars, they dig burrows under the desert sand to hide away from the hot sun.

burrowing owl

eastern indigo snake

Underground they are also protected from skunks and other predators such as snakes. When the tortoises leave, their burrows may become homes for as many as 360 different types of animals, including burrowing owls.

BANDED SNAILS also have a ready-made home. These soft-bodied animals are known as molluscs and they live in Europe. Unlike their close relatives, the slugs, these snails grow beautiful, spiralled shells.

They can pull their soft bodies into their armoured homes when they're in danger of being eaten by birds or other animals.

In winter months the snails hibernate inside their shells. They form a dried layer of mucus across the entrance to stop themselves drying out.

The master house-builders of the bird world live in South America. **RED OVEN BIRDS** feast on snails and insects, but sometimes they become food for snakes, birds of prey and even domestic cats.

To keep their chicks safe, the parents build dome-shaped nests that look like little ovens.

egg chamber

entrance

dividing wall

It can take the adult birds months to make the nests using mud or clay mixed with hair or straw. A narrow entrance leads to a divided space, with the cosy egg chamber lined with soft grass and feathers.

NORTH AMERICAN PILEATED WOODPECKERS are the carpenters of the bird world. They care for their young inside large hollows that they chisel out of dead or decaying trees with their powerful beaks. The leftover wood shavings create a soft carpet inside the chamber.

The birds defend their home
area, or territory, all year round
by drumming loudly on trees.
They attack other birds that
try to steal their nest sites.

The **NORTH AMERICAN BEAVER** is the second largest rodent on Earth. These intelligent animals live partly on land and partly in the water. They are famous for building wooden dams across rivers and lakes.

The beavers cut down trees by gnawing through them with their front teeth. Then they drag the logs into position on the water. They collect rocks and mud in their paws and pack everything together to make a watertight lodge.

nesting chamber

dam

eating chamber

underwater
entrance

The lodges have underwater entrances that lead
to eating and nesting areas. Sometimes lodges
connect to burrows in the sides of riverbanks.

In the seas around Indonesia, the amazing eel-like **STAR PEARLFISH** hides from its enemies in some very weird places! The leopard sea cucumber lives on the sea floor. It has no nose, so it breathes through its bottom, which relaxes as it breathes out. When this happens, star pearlfish take the chance to swim inside!

Now that you've learnt about so many unusual and interesting animal homes, perhaps you can try to find some when you are out and about near your own home.

DISCOVER MORE

BANDED SNAILS

These snails can fool their predators by looking different from one another. Some are pink, some yellow and some brown. Some have one stripe, some three and some six. This means that the snails are more difficult for predators to find and, even if all the yellow ones get eaten, the pink ones will survive.

BARN OWLS

Barn owls are able to hunt mice and other animals in the total darkness of a farmyard at night thanks to their superb hearing – the most sensitive of any animal ever tested! Their ears are positioned diagonally from each other and this helps their brain pinpoint exactly where their prey is when it is scurrying around beneath them.

BLACK-AND-WHITE RUFFED LEMURS

This lemur and all the other types of lemur live on the island of Madagascar, off the coast of Africa. The word 'lemur' means 'ghost' in the native Malagasy language. Strange meat-eating mammals, called fossas, climb trees to hunt lemurs, and the lemurs are also hunted and eaten by people, so many species are now very rare.

CORALS

Corals are animals that are related to sea anemones and jellyfish. At the base of a hard coral is a rock-like skeleton. When thousands of hard corals come together they build reefs that act as a support for other animals. Australia's Great Barrier Reef is the world's biggest single structure made by living creatures. However, this particular reef is now under threat from human activities such as oil spills in the sea.

DARWIN'S BARK SPIDERS

The silk of the Darwin's bark spider is one of the toughest natural materials known on Earth. For its size, it is stronger than steel and yet it is highly elastic, which means it can absorb massive amounts of energy before it will break. People have tried, but are not yet able to re-create such a tough fibre.

GOPHER TORTOISES

Gopher tortoises have special shovel-like front legs that are excellent for digging the large, deep burrows they use for shelter. You can tell the difference between male and female gopher tortoises by the shape of the underside of their shells. The males' shells are concave, curving inwards, while the females' shells are flat.

HERMIT CRABS

These crabs live on the seashore and, as they grow, look for ever larger abandoned sea shells to climb into. They are crustaceans, belonging to the same group of animals as lobsters and prawns. Hermit crabs can live up to 30 years in the wild.

HONEY BEES

Honey bees perform dances to tell each other how far away and exactly where flowers are so they can all go there to collect nectar. A very excited 'waggle dance' indicates lots of tasty nectar, and hundreds of bees will gather to watch. It takes eight bees all of their lives to make just one teaspoon of delicious honey!

NORTH AMERICAN BEAVERS

North American beavers are known as 'ecosystem engineers' because their activities change the habitats in which they live. By damming steams and rivers, they create ponds of still water where vegetation grows and animal life flourishes. The beavers also help prevent flooding because their dams store the water and release it to flow downstream more slowly.

NORTH AMERICAN PILEATED WOODPECKERS

Pileated woodpeckers hammer their beaks into tough wood up to 12,000 times a day. They can do this without getting a headache because the special shape of their beak sends vibrations away from the brain. They also have very strong neck muscles and reduced space around the brain that stops it banging around when they are pecking wood.

PORCUPINES

Porcupines are rodents and related to beavers. Their bodies are covered in 30,000 sharp quills made from keratin, the same material as your hair and fingernails. They defend themselves by sticking these sharp weapons into predators. Then they grow new ones, so they are always armed.

RED OVEN BIRDS

These songbirds have discovered how to benefit from the ways in which humans have changed their natural habitat, often building their circular mud nests on top of fence posts or on houses. They feed mainly on beetles, crickets, ants and spiders.

SNOW LEOPARDS

Snow leopards live in the snowy mountain ranges of central Asia. They have huge furry paws that act like snowshoes, spreading their weight so they can walk without sinking into the snow. The extra thick skin on their paw pads prevents them from being cut on sharp rocks when they chase prey.

STAR PEARLFISH

Star pearlfish are able to live inside sea cucumbers because the pearlfish release a slimy protective substance called mucus onto their skin. The mucus helps the fish tolerate the poisons that sea cucumbers release inside their bodies. They make up to ten times more of this mucus than fish that don't live in such unpleasant places!

TERMITES

For every human on Earth there is the equivalent of a cow's weight of termites! Up to a million of these insects can live in one single colony. Kings, queens, workers and soldiers live together and communicate using chemical scents called 'pheromones'. Young kings and queens have wings and can fly. They leave their colonies to make new homes.